PRAISE FOR
FROM THE PROJECTS TO THE BOARDROOM

The world is starving for LOVE, HOPE, HEALING, ENCOURAGEMENT, and DIRECTION at a time of unrest. My friend Joe Humphries takes us on a journey in his book *From the Projects to The Boardroom*, where God guides him from poverty to redemption. Raised by a loving single mother, she encouraged her son living in government housing that he can be anything he desires if he puts God first in his life. I have witnessed Joe going into very troubled cities around this nation and making a positive impact by serving others. If you want real-life change, this is the book.
Frank Harrison, Chairman & Chief Executive Officer of Coca-Cola Consolidated, Inc.

This is a book you will not be able to put down. What a wonderful story of faith, hope, and love. Prepare yourself to shed some tears, but also know there will be moments of joy that will make you want to shout!
Dr. Daniel L. Akin, President of Southeastern Baptist Theological Seminary

If you grew up without a dad, please read this book. Joe Humphries captures so well the devastation that an absentee father brings, and yet he tells us a greater story of redemption. A faithful, hardworking, loving, and praying mom. A mentor he eventually called Dad. And a stranger in the airport who laid bare Joe's deepest longing. Behind these and other people in Joe's life stands a God who plucked him from the projects and placed him in the boardroom—and then called him to share that story with you and me. This story of grief and loss, hope and healing puts on radiant display the love and faithfulness of our true Father, who will never leave us or forsake us.

Dr. Russell L. Meek, Adjunct Instructor of Hebrew and Old Testament, Moody Theological and Visiting Professor of Old Testament, William Tennent School of Theology

From the Projects to the Boardroom is an inspiring and honest account of the difficult but rewarding task of taking what life gives you, entrusting it to God, and making the most of it. In it, the author takes us on a moving journey through childhood adversity, marriage, business success, burnout, restoration, and victorious living. Heartfelt, honest, and wise. Take notice: this son of a gun is a home run.

Dr. Bruce Riley Ashford, author of Letters to an American Christian and The Gospel of Our King

Nearly twenty-five years ago I met Joe and knew immediately that he was special. He was bold, vocal, and a go-getter. What I did not learn until years later was the motivation behind the man. Joe grew up with a loving mother and an absentee dad who repeatedly broke his heart. What man broke, however, the Master Potter used to construct a Christian giant. From the project to the boardroom, from the football field to the stage, Joe has a story that will inspire, uplift, motivate, and cause each of us to reevaluate how effectively we are using our God-given gifts to better this world.

Asa L. Bell, Jr. Principal at The Law Office of Asa L. Bell & Certified Superior Mediator

From Lee Walker Heights to the heights of corporate America, Joe leaves you inspired to be a better person, father, spouse, and Christian. *From the Projects to the Boardroom* is an amazing reminder of how powerful words are, especially the word HOPE.

Andy Crawford, CEO of Outgo360

From the Projects to the Boardroom is a reminder of how staying the course brings life-changing experiences to the ones we love most. Every word is directly from Joe's heart, and you will feel it as you read it. Get ready for your hearts to be changed and challenged at a time when hope and encouragement are missing throughout this world.

Scott Edwards, CEO and President of Broader Exposure

This book is a must read—you will truly walk a mile in someone else's shoes at a time in our nation's history when we need empathy more than ever before. Joe Humphries allows his personal story to speak to a subject matter that is so relevant for the times in which we live. As I consider his book, two words come to mind: authentic and transparent. Joe allows his story to provide hope and healing to the reader, reminding us that all things work together for good for those who love God and are called according to His purpose.

Larry Griffith, CEO of Corporate Chaplains of America

Joe's life is an amazing journey that started in a single-parent home in a housing project and led to the upper echelons of corporate executive life. Along the way, Joe dealt with much pain and learned many hard lessons that later helped mold his success. He has now dedicated his life to helping others overcome their struggles and achieve more than they could ever imagine. A gifted speaker and storyteller, Joe shares his story in *From the Projects to the Boardroom,* a book that will encourage and inspire all who read it.

Steve Grissom, Founder and CEO of Church Initiative Publishing Company

I love great stories, especially about a likable underdog. But when you take authentic personal stories about overcoming all odds and you pair them with solid, biblical applications to real life, you have a winning combination! Joe's blending of storytelling and life application is life changing. In his book, *From the Projects to the Boardroom*, he hits the target and points people to the God he knows so well.

Chris Patton, CEO of His Way at Work

I had the privilege of coaching Joe Humphries, who was an outstanding football player and leader on and off the field. He played major roles in helping his high school football team win back-to-back Western 4A Conference championships during his junior and senior years. *From the Projects to the Boardroom* is a compelling story about a young man who grew up in government housing; the book takes you on a journey and shows how lessons learned in athletics played a major role and drew a road map for him to become successful in life and business. Get ready to be inspired, encouraged, and hopeful about the future.

Coach (Pete) Bruce Peterson

Congratulations, you've made a good choice. Reading about Joe's journey or, better yet, hearing him tell it, will give inspiration and practical steps to capture your dream. You will be moved as you hear how Joe discovered God's path and power to break from childhood poverty and wounds to become an influential business and Christian leader.

Larry Wilson, Founder and Director of Lighthouse Ministries Christian Counseling

Fantastic book. If you think the American dream is dead, you need to read this book. Joe demonstrates that no matter what your background or circumstances are, you can be a success in life.

Ed O'Brien, Founder and CEO of Atlantic Custom Containers

Let your heart be encouraged by this story of a mom's vision for her child that was powered by faith. The practical pearls you will catch from reading Joe's life story will make every relationship you have richer.

Dr. Charlie Vittitow, Missions Pastor at Southeast Christian Church, Louisville, KY

From the Projects to the Boardroom is a great read. It is an inspiring story of hope, forgiveness, and the power of a dream. It will encourage you to not only survive tough times but to thrive. Joe's story reaffirms the impact a praying parent can have on a child's life.

Keith Conley, Director of Financial Aid at Western Piedmont Community College (Retired)

When I met Joe fifteen years ago, I recognized that God clearly has His hand on him. I believed some amazing things were in store for Joe's future, and I was right. He is a man of integrity with a heart to hear and follow God's voice. Joe's story relatable to everyone; it is the gospel of Jesus Christ fleshed out in a man's life. This book will rekindle your faith, inspire hope, and encourage you to rise up and pursue the God who loves you and the life He desires to give you.

Chuck Milian, Senior Pastor at Crossroads Fellowship (retired) and CEO and Founder of Milian Enterprises, Raleigh, NC

The day that I met Joe Humphries was a memorable one. I was making a sales call in his office, and he made an impromptu speech that I will never forget. It was a speech that showed a deep understanding of faith and a gift to communicate. It has been a real pleasure getting to know Joe. His journey has inspired me, and I am certain that his book, *From the Projects to the Boardroom*, will have the same effect on readers.

J. D. Ross, Founder and CEO of Circle of the Panda

I am honored to be an ongoing recipient of Joe's coaching and mentoring. The story God continues to write into his life has painted a powerful perspective for me. I am excited for the masses to read his amazing story of hope. Through this book, you will meet the man of God behind the story. Joe will draw you in with his honesty, humility, passion, and encouragement. By the end of the story, you will be convinced that God is not done with you. The message of hope infused on every page is greatly needed and cannot be heard often enough.

Jordan Johnson, Senior Pastor, Antioch Baptist Church, Lovelady, TX

Joe reminds us that we are not alone in our struggles. His words will inspire and lift you up as he shares his life's challenges. Joe teaches us that compassion, grace, and humility are not weaknesses but are strengths that we must learn to live a fulfilling life.

Carl DeTorres CEO of Flex Logistics, Orange County, CA

It has been an honor and privilege to call Joe a friend and business associate for the last fifteen years. He has written a book that you will want to share with your family and friends. *From the Projects to the Boardroom* is a story about determination, perseverance, and faith, and it is certainly a breath of fresh air. This book highlights what it means to be a person of strength and conviction. Joe's sense of humility is truly inspirational, and his uplifting personality and positive attitude infuse this heartfelt story.

Mike Howard, CEO and Owner, Polymer Southeast

Joe's story is powerful! It's a clear example of God's blessings when people yield to Him. Joe's transparency also highlights God's faithfulness. Struggles in life are real for all of us, and this book leads us to the true source of hope by pointing us to God's Word.

Jeremy Porras, Executive Director of the Raleigh Dream Center

From the Projects to the Boardroom is a powerful and inspirational journey. This book will encourage you to push through tough times. Joe's honesty and openness about his own pain and healing give light and hope to anyone reading this incredible book.

Andy George, Senior Pastor Crossroads Fellowship

FROM THE PROJECTS TO THE BOARDROOM

A Little Boy's Journey out of Poverty, Led by a God Who Never Let Go of His Hand.

BY JOE HUMPHRIES

From the Projects to the Boardroom:
A Little Boy's Journey out of Poverty,
Led by a God Who Never Let Go of His Hand

 **LEGACY MEDIA**

Wake Forest, NC

ISBN-13: 978-0-578-33363-2

Printed in the USA

I dedicate this book to my mother, Mildred Humphries. Mom, by God's grace, we made it out of the projects!

CONTENTS

FOREWORD

Joe is a wonderful Christian brother who enjoyed a very successful career in business that culminated in him serving as a senior executive for a large multinational company headquartered in Italy. For many years he led their US headquarters and largest operations in North America. This might not be so remarkable except for the fact that Joe was raised in the tough projects of Asheville, NC, by a Christian single mom. In other words, Joe is a great example of a black youth that overcame exceptionally long odds to make it to the pinnacle of business success.

I knew Joe years before we entered into a close mentoring relationship over five years ago. However, our relationship accelerated further after he felt God calling him to step away from his life in the executive ranks and start a ministry to bring Christ's hope and healing to men and boys who started out in life just as he did. His ministry is called 3C Leadership. The "3C" stands for the number the government placed on the apartment in the projects where he was raised.

A number of business and ministry leaders encouraged Joe to write a book about his experience of transformation from the projects to the boardroom. Once again, we all observed Joe's willingness to listen to counsel, yet sought God's blessing first and foremost before agreeing to embark on the journey. Only after he was convinced God was on board with the idea did the writing process begin in earnest.

Joe possesses excellent skills as a communicator, be it on the platform, in the community, or one on one. Joe has a life-changing message of hope and inspiration that, in his own words, only the true God of the universe can provide. By all means read this book and then share it with someone unlike you—be prepared to see God at work, possibly as you have never seen before.

In addition to many church and civic commitments, Joe also serves on the national board of directors for the publishing company Church Initiative. Joe and his wonderful wife of thirty-four years, Janet, have one grown daughter, Danielle, who works in the Wake County education system.

Yes, Joe Humphries is the *real deal*, and his story, as illustrated within the pages of this book, exemplify what God will do with a life totally submitted to His will. Anyone reading this book will walk away encouraged and better for the time spent with it. Certainly, God has raised up a man like Joe for just a time as we now live in and has gifted him to reach across all ethnic, economic, racial, faith and non-faith communities with a special message of hope and healing.

Dr. Mark Cress, Founder, Corporate Chaplains of America

ACKNOWLEDGEMENTS

Writing this book has been an experience unlike any other. It has caused me to reach back and think of people and experiences that were instrumental in the development of who I am today. I embrace my assignment from God, and my goal for this book (and the rest of my life) is to share His Word in order to bring healing and encouragement to all who will accept it. I want to challenge a dark world in which too many people make God small or believe He has lost His power.

May the testimony shared within this book make it abundantly clear that God still holds this world in the palm of His hand! He has *all* power to do what He wants to do, when and for whom He wants to do it. Let it further be known that God is in full control and is coming back for a church without spot or wrinkle. May we all get ready and stay ready for His return.

I extend special thanks to each person who has invested in my life. Your love and many acts of kindness throughout the years will never be forgotten.

Most deeply, I want to thank my dear wife of thirty-four years, Janet, and my precious daughter, Danielle, for their unconditional love and support. Through sunny days and dark nights, they encouraged me to stay focused on the right path. I also thank them for the many times they sit and listen to me speak; even though they know my story word for word by now, they always make it seem like they are hearing it for the first time!

God has blessed me with many men who have mentored me and invested in my life. I would like to acknowledge a few of them here:

Walter Wells: My childhood barber and very first mentor;

Coach Bruce Peterson: My high school football coach;

Hersey Hall: My first business mentor;

Keith Conely: My best man for one day but a brother for life;

Asa Bell, Jr: A friend who has stuck closer than a brother;

Joe Fernandez: A man who mentored me and whom I called dad;

Darryl High: A man that will come help you whether it's 3:00pm or 3:00am;

Winford Barr: A man that walked with me during my dark season;

Larry Wilson: A man whom God used in such a critical point in my life;

Chuck Milian: A pastor who has invested and helped prepare me for this season; and

Dr. Mark Cress: A man who has invested in me and who challenged me to burn my boats of safety to answer my call from God.

The words of Isaac Newton ring true of these men: "If I have seen further than others, it is by standing upon the shoulders of giants." Thank you to all the "giants" in my life who have allowed me to stand on their shoulders.

Finally, thank you to the contributing book editors: Lisa Haynes, Founder of Chromawords; David Brass, CEO of Inbound Ink; and Angela Ross Bell.

CHAPTER # 1
A MOTHER PRAYING IN THE WINDOW

Many people imagine a childhood spent living in the projects as one of constant deprivation and misery. Tragically, that is the story for far too many children. Growing up in a single-parent household with six siblings was incredibly challenging in countless ways. But my family had something special that turned the odds in our favor: we had Mildred Humphries as our mother.

Because of my mom, the first twenty-one years of my life—spent in government housing—were full of love, encouragement and plenty of grace. Despite our physical poverty, my mother's rich faith and continual prayers paved the way for my eventual success in life.

Our apartment—number 3C in Lee Walker Heights—was in the projects of Asheville, North Carolina. It had only one first-floor window, in the kitchen. It was this solitary window where my mother often stood, keeping an eye on her children and offering continual prayers. She personalized the well-known verse, Philippians 4:13, for me: "Joe, you can do all things through Christ which strengthens you. You are special. I believe in you. If you are obedient to God and live a life honoring him, one day you will be successful. You will also be a loving husband and the present father that you do not have."

Of my mom's seven children, I was the youngest. Her sacrifices for us were endless, her prayers without ceasing. My eyes still fill with tears as I think of my mom's unrelenting love for me. To this day, she is the hardest-working person I have ever known. In addition to working a full-time job, she cleaned houses for extra income to ensure she could provide for us. In the winter she walked to work with holes in her shoes so that her children didn't have to have holes in theirs.

She never missed a single one of my home football games. Although my mom knew nothing about football—and she probably couldn't wait for the games to be over—she never left early, even in rain or sleet. Occasionally I looked into the stands during terrible weather and saw her sitting there. Out of concern, I hoped that she would go home and get warm and dry, but she always stayed in her seat until the game ended. That's an authentic example of a mother's love.

LIFE LESSONS IN MORAL INTEGRITY

Sometimes my mom and I rode the bus and walked to the houses she was hired to clean. I loved joining her because she had the gift of making anything fun, even work. Pretending that the children's rooms in the beautiful homes belonged to me was wonderful. Walking through the spacious rooms, I fantasized about living in a beautiful, safe neighborhood.

My mom noticed me admiring the bedrooms and said, "Joe, what are you thinking about?"

"I am thinking about these rooms being mine," I replied.

"You'll have a house with rooms even nicer than these one day," she said. "You'll be able to pay someone to clean your house. Remember to be good to them."

Then she went back to her cleaning duties. She showed me by example how to treat people the right way.

Another lesson my mom taught me was the importance of being my own man. Some of the neighborhood children teased my siblings and me because my mom required us to attend church services regularly. If that wasn't bad enough, my church was featured on a television show every Sunday morning called *Count on Me*. On the show, my third eldest sister, my mom, and I sang in the choir.

Sometimes the host picked me to pray on the show. The next day at school, some of my classmates often laughed at me.

The humiliation made me want to quit the show, but my mom wouldn't allow it. She emphasized that there will always be people who ridicule you, even when you accomplish great things. To be my own man, she explained, I had to confront this mockery head-on and not allow anyone to define who I was.

As I grew into adolescence, my mom continued to pour into my life with constant affirmations, always telling me that God had a special plan for my life. She asked me if I believed that God was calling me to speak His Word. I made many attempts to ignore her question! As I got older, she kept asking the same question, and I kept avoiding it. But deep inside my heart, even as a child, I knew God was calling me to speak His Word. And Mom did too. I just wasn't ready to answer His call yet.

To my mom, discipline in academics was a non-negotiable. To prove it, one of her absolute rules was for her children to be home before the streetlights came on—not just for safety but to make sure we completed our homework. She was so adamant about our academic success that she went to every PTA meeting, school play, and parent conference, even though she didn't have a driver's license or vehicle to get there. One of her favorite pieces of advice was, "having nothing is not an excuse for doing nothing," and she personified that mindset in countless ways.

I'm sure mother attended far more school-related meetings than she wanted to because I constantly got in trouble during my elementary-school years. Unfortunately, time-out was not a popular disciplinary option in those days, but my mom had other ways of getting my attention. I can honestly say that nothing else straightened up my act like the corrections she loved me enough to administer.

GIVING BACK TO THE WOMAN WHO GAVE ME SO MUCH

Since childhood I'd dreamed of caring for my mother financially. As I grew into a young man, I finally got that chance. I began sending her money each month to make sure I met her needs—with a little extra for splurges. Some of the best moments of my life have been returning home to Asheville and taking her shopping.

On one of these trips to the shopping mall, our goal was to find a white pair of shoes she needed to serve communion at her church. I noticed her staring at a pair of gold shoes, and I asked her if she wanted them.

"No, you're already buying me the white shoes," she replied.

I immediately had a flashback of her walking to work in the winter with holes in her shoes. I asked the salesperson to bring out the gold shoes to try on. Once my mom placed the shoes on her feet, she got up and walked around. I asked her how the shoes felt.

"These are the most comfortable shoes that I've ever had on my feet," she said.

That settled it. "We're going to buy both pairs," I said.

She refused my offer, suggesting that they were far too expensive.

My reaction was immediate, and it was one of the few times in my life I've gotten impatient with my mom.

"We're buying both—there is no other option," I said.

I told the salesperson we would take both pairs. I confidently announced to my mother that this was how things were going to be. *This moment with my mom was a blessing from God that I will cherish for the rest of my life. To this day, I still make a point of getting back to Asheville to schedule regular shopping trips with my mom—including a stop first at Starbucks for hot chocolate and conversation. This is our special time together as we reflect on how far God has brought us.*

FOUR WAYS TO USE YOUR INFLUENCE AS A MOTHER

My encouragement to mothers, especially single mothers, is to never underestimate your power. I did not experience the validation of a loving relationship with my father, but my mom's love, prayers, and encouragement helped close the deficit. Some of the most powerful experiences of my childhood were when I heard my mother praying for me. She didn't realize how deeply her private petitions to God penetrated my heart and mind.

Our outward circumstances were poverty and deprivation at apartment 3C, but Mom's words and actions imprinted optimistic hope deep within her baby boy's heart. Her unconditional love enabled me to reach goals beyond my wildest dreams.

I recently had a conversation with my mom in which she said,

"I'm sorry that I didn't have much to give you."

"You have given me love and prayers that are immeasurable," I replied. "You introduced me to God, and He has honored you by blessing me because of your prayers. What else is left for you to give me?"

Mothers, God has given you the power to foster your children's dreams, regardless of their circumstances. The Bible shares a promising story of Jesus's response to a grieving mother in Luke 7:11–15. It reads:

Soon afterward, Jesus went to a town called Nain, and his disciples and a large crowd went along with him. As he approached the town gate, a dead person was being carried out—the only son of his mother, and she was a widow. And a large crowd from the town was with her. When the Lord saw her, His heart went out to her, and He said, "Don't cry." Then He went up and touched the coffin, and those carrying it stood still. He said, "Young man, I say to you, get up!" The dead man sat up and began to talk, and Jesus gave him back to his mother.

This mother's situation was heartbreaking. She had already suffered the loss of her husband. Now her only son was dead. Plagued with hardships, she relied on her son for financial support. This woman was probably past her childbearing years and would most likely not remarry. This mother was dealing with an impossible storm, and Jesus knew this. Her *love and compassion for her son moved Jesus to act on her behalf.*

You, too, might be dealing with the storms of life, but Jesus knows every detail about you and what you are going through. Here are four ways to use your unique role as a mother to bless your children:

1. Begin with Forgiveness

Mothers, your future and your children's futures begin with forgiveness. This is especially important for single moms. My mother made mistakes, but she made it clear that I wasn't one of them. She understood the significance of forgiving the people in our lives who had wronged us, beginning with my dad.

> Be kind and compassionate to one another, forgiving each other, just as in Christ God forgave you. (Ephesians 4:32)

> For if you forgive men when they sin against you, your heavenly Father will also forgive you. But if you do not forgive men their sins, your Father will not forgive your sins. (Matthew 6:14–15)

Forgiveness means giving up the right to hurt someone who hurt you. Satan wants you to hold grudges that rot away your soul. The danger in an unforgiving heart is that we spend more time being bitter when we should be better.

Understand that your children are fully aware of your unwillingness to forgive. They know when you hold grudges and won't release bitterness. Once you've discovered your value and have acted upon God's command to forgive others, you can move forward with new-found hope and optimism. The future for you and your children will become brighter.

> For I know the plans I have for you, declares the Lord, plans to prosper you and not to harm you, plans to give you hope and a future. (Jeremiah 29:11)

I implore you to stop where you are right now and ask God to forgive you for any unconfessed sins. I also encourage you to take a moment to forgive those who have hurt you.

2. Understand Your Value

You must know your importance and value to God. If you don't grasp this truth, your children's growth and development throughout life will be hindered. By understanding your own value, your children will better understand theirs.

Emphasize to your children that their existence is intentional, even before their earthly arrival. God set the blueprint for their lives with meticulous detail, noting each moment of their lives from beginning to end. As Jeremiah 1:5a says, "Before I formed you in the womb I knew you, before you were born I set you apart."

3. Love and Discipline Your Child

Your child's strong disposition might have you at a loss. It probably seems you can't do anything to help them. But that is a lie of

Satan—he wants you to feel alone and hopeless. He wants you to believe that your child is the only one misbehaving. Please realize this is not the case. There were seasons in my life when I continually challenged my mother, even earning the nickname "Little Bad Joe." I believe there were many days when Jesus reassured my mom with the truth that He had a plan for me.

One reason that plan came to fruition is that my mother corrected my rebelliousness. Pray for your children and love them, but don't ignore their disobedience and do discipline them as needed. I am confident that God has plans for your children too.

4. Pray and Fast

For many mothers, the storms of life are so strong they can't see a way out. While there are many ways of escape from the storm, fasting is one practice my mother used time and time again.

Fasting is abstaining from something you would normally do, such as eating and drinking, for a set period of time. The purpose is to take your focus off of your self—your appetites and emotions—and focus intently on God.

Fasting allows God to more fully capture your attention, and it has the power to bring forth spiritual growth and healing to your soul. There is something special about a mother fasting on behalf of her children. I believe God honors mothers when they fast.

In the Bible, Hannah fasted because she was barren and desperately wanted a child. She cried out to God, and He heard her plea. God honored Hannah by blessing her with a son, the prophet

Samuel. I remember my mother always saying, "I fasted for you."

Is it possible to miss your greatest breakthroughs because of an unwillingness to fast?

Sometimes life's storms are fearsome. They cause us to remain idle because we fear the unknown. This happened when the disciples found themselves stuck in the middle of a terrible storm at sea (Matthew 14). As Jesus approached their boat, they were so spooked they thought He was a ghost! But Jesus arrived at the right moment with the right solution. He told the disciples, "It is I, don't be afraid."

Jesus offers us the same solution today.

God's presence will calm the storms in your life—whether they are outside the boat or inside your heart—because He *loves* and *values* you. When you give your storms to Jesus, He guides you to safe, solid ground just as He did with His disciples.

Fasting helps us to see the scars in our soul that, in the busyness of daily life, we rarely see. Emotional scars that we've neglected keep us stuck in our storms. But when we draw near to God, we magnify Him. Soon our fears diminish, and our peace is restored. The storms calm down and the scars can be healed.

A while ago I heard a story about a woman who moved back to her hometown to purchase her childhood home. The land needed reclamation after her mother and father had passed away. One of her first tasks was to hire someone to clean out the well her father dug many years before. Over time, debris and garbage had been tossed into the well, rendering it useless for water. Initially, the cleaning crew dug out a gigantic pile of garbage, but the woman told them to keep digging. Finally, after three days of work, the woman looked at the heaping pile of trash and declared, "You're done."

Puzzled, one of the men asked how she knew the job was complete. She answered, "Because after papa dug the well, when I was a little girl, I took a teapot and threw it in. I figured the first thing that went into the well would be the last thing that came out."

Fasting allows the Holy Spirit to come in. And just like those well diggers, God will dig out the clutter. You will have a hard time accepting the grace and forgiveness of the Lord if you haven't gotten down to that "teapot" in your own heart. You must extract that first offense you put in the pile years ago. You may have to dig for a long time, but once you reach that teapot, the river of living water can spring back up out of you and refresh your soul.

THANK YOU, MOM!

Thank you, Mom, for praying and fasting for me and helping me to understand my value in becoming the godly man that I am. May God continue to bless you at eighty-nine years young! As I write this book, I cannot thank you enough for your love, prayers, encouragement, and sacrifices. I pray that God pours His grace over you.

Mothers, you can entrust your unknown future to a known God. Finally, understand that you and God are more than enough for your children!

REFLECTION

Share your thoughts below with God about how you can pray, fast, and encourage your children. What could be blocking God from working? Are you ready to get to that teapot?

_____

_____

_____

_____

_____

_____

_____

_____

_____

_____

_____

_____

_____

_____

_____

_____

_____

_____

_____

_____

_____

_____

_____

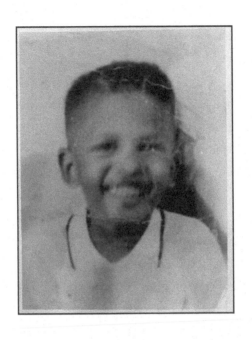

CHAPTER # 2
THE LITTLE BOY WHO DREAMED ON THE STEPS OF 3C LEE WALKER HEIGHTS

Sirens, arguments, and gunshots. Those were the major chords in the noisy soundtrack of my neighborhood. From the steps of my apartment, I often watched police officers break up fights or arrest my neighbors. I saw paramedics pick up stabbing or gunshot victims. The chaos was stressful and fearful, but it was the only environment I knew.

I had one escape as a young boy: daydreaming. I used my imagination to fantasize about the impossible and envision a life far beyond where I sat. The journeys I took in my daydreams became my favorite pastime.

I liked to visualize myself as a successful business executive earning $50,000 a year—a staggering amount to me at the time—so I could take care of my family. This impressive salary would spare my own children from having to grow up in a poverty-stricken neighborhood like I did. My dreams extended to helping my mom escape the projects and move into a house. I remember many times when tears rolled down my face uncontrollably at these thoughts.

When I wasn't daydreaming about becoming a successful businessperson, I enjoyed tuning into sports on the television. Wrestling was one of my favorites. I loved watching the feats and antics of my generation's legends: Chief Wahoo McDaniel, Paul Jones, Ricky Steamboat, and the incomparable Rick Flair, "The Nature Boy." I imagined being a wrestler and winning the world championship title. Other times I pretended to be a football player, winning the game by making the last tackle or intercepting the ball and running it back for the final touchdown. The basketball court was another stage I saw myself performing on: I dribbled the ball to the hoop and made the game-winning shot, celebrating with my teammates and a stadium filled with cheering fans.

GOD'S VOICE IN MY LIFE

Whether it was making a good living or excelling in sports, my imaginings were all about escaping to become something more. One of my real-life inspirations came from an insurance company at the bottom of the hill in my neighborhood. The owner paid a friend and me to clean his office building. I admired that he was a successful businessman, but even more I admired how he treated his customers with care and how kindly he treated me. Although he didn't know it at the time, this man taught me my earliest lessons about doing business the right way.

I didn't realize it until later, but daydreaming was also a way for me to spend quality time with God. He used those opportunities to share His plans for my life with me. The stair steps of apartment 3C became the place where I sat and listened to God's voice, a haven where He provided insight into my future. As I grew older and busier with life, days, weeks, and sometimes months flew by before I got back to those stair steps and spent time with God once more.

The steps of a good man are ordered by the Lord, And He delights in his way.
Though he falls, he shall not be utterly cast down. (Psalm 37:23–24)

HOW GOD HELPED ME ESCAPE THE PROJECTS

Even though my aspirations were about becoming a successful business executive or professional athlete, one call kept resurfacing—to speak God's Word. No matter how much I tried to escape it, there it was. I knew God had a calling on my life, but I didn't know how to deal with it. I had no desire to teach or speak God's Word. This tension would once again cause tears to stream down my face.

Later in life I came to an important conclusion: God enabled me to daydream to give me hope. There was a load of discouragement in my surroundings, and that reality was often painfully disheartening. But the world of my dreams was much different. God used my desires—my vision of becoming a businessman, achieving more, and ultimately serving Him—to escape the temptation of destruction that surrounded me in the projects.

God used more than my imagination, of course—he also used my mother's fervent prayers and my fear of letting her down. These elements combined to keep me far from the path of the neighborhood drug dealers and other bad things that I could have gotten into. Unfortunately, many of my friends chose that route. God's grace alone kept me from it. God used my youth in the projects to mature me, to help me rely solely on Him. From these troubled surroundings I learned countless lessons that helped me triumph in life.

My dreams motivated me. Those desires gave little Joe hope. ***Wrestling might be fake, but I knew that God was real.*** I had no clue how I would escape the projects, become a success in business, meet and marry a godly and beautiful woman, and have a healthy family life with children. But I knew God was—and *is*—able to do abundantly above anything I ever dreamed for myself.

REMEMBERING WHERE I CAME FROM

Often, on trips back to Asheville to visit my mom, I drove out of my way to pass through my old neighborhood and visit my apartment, gazing at the stair steps where I once sat and daydreamed. Before my apartment was torn down, my sister Deborah and I took my wife and daughter to the apartment we grew up in. It was special to see my daughter's face as she looked through the window of our apartment. The complex has since been demolished, but the memories will always be with me. I'm forever indebted to God for His grace and mercy in how far He has brought me since my childhood in Lee Walker Heights.

During our roughest times my mother reminded me not to focus on where I am but to focus on where God is taking me. One of the many ways God illustrates His love is through the way mothers encourage their children amid life's toughest circumstances. I'm grateful for the moments that God allowed me to dream on the steps of my childhood apartment. As I reminisce on my childhood, I realize how blessed and protected I was, much more than I could see so many years ago.

REFLECTION

How has God held your hand and allowed you to dream? W
has the Lord revealed to you in those moments about His plans f
your life? Is anything keeping you from believing Him? Share you
thoughts below.

_____

_____

_____

_____

_____

_____

_____

_____

_____

_____

_____

_____

_____

_____

_____

_____

_____

_____

_____

_____

CHAPTER # 3
FATHERLESS BUT NOT FORSAKEN

A father to the fatherless, a defender of widows, is God in his holy dwelling. (Psalm 68:5)

When a father does not show up or keep his word, it may seem like a minor detail to him. But those disappointments can loom so large to his child that they are never forgotten.

For me, it was the haircut I did not get.

One morning, when I was ten or twelve and it was back-to-school time, my mother told me my dad was coming to take me for a haircut. Joy and anticipation filled my heart! Seeing my father was all I could think about that day at school.

I was so excited to go to the barbershop with my dad. When the school bus let me off, I ran home, put my books up, changed clothes, and then plopped myself down on the front steps of our apartment to wait.

"Do you want a snack, Joe?" my mom asked.

"No thanks," I replied. I rarely passed up a chance to eat, but I was so eager to see my father that food was not my priority.

An hour went by. I kept a sharp lookout for my dad's car, which I knew well: a gray stick-shift Oldsmobile with black leather seats. No matter how many cars went by, I'd tell myself his would be the next one. It wasn't until a couple hours later that my mom finally came to me with sadness in her eyes and said, "Joseph, I don't believe your father is coming tonight. You should come in and eat."

That day my relationship with my father changed. Until then, I held out hope that he would become the great dad I always dreamed of. I lived for the rare occasions he spent time with me, and I admired how well he dressed, especially his wingtip dress shoes (a style of shoe I still wear to this day).

But now, seeing the pain and anguish in my mother's face, I felt angry with him for the first time. My desire to hug him turned into an urge to punch him in the nose! It was one thing to hurt me, but causing my mother to suffer crossed the line. Father or not, I could not tolerate anyone upsetting her.

Unfortunately, my dad did not show up that day or any other day.

NEARBY BUT FAR AWAY

From that point on I stopped trusting what my father said. And sadly, time and time again his actions lengthened my list of reasons not to believe him.

I longed for a kind, attentive father and couldn't understand why he didn't love me. During my football games at school, I saw the way my teammates' dads were there to tell them how well they played. Those dads hugged their sons and said they were proud of them.

Even though my dad lived just two red lights from my football stadium, he never came to see my games. His house was just outside the boundaries of the projects where we lived. Every day on the way to and from middle school I walked by his beautiful home and wondered how amazing it would be to live there. But I knew I was not welcome to even knock on his door. His neighborhood and mine were a world apart. He had a fine home and several cars, but we lived in poverty.

I cannot imagine my daughter not being welcome at my house. In fact, I've given her a key to my house so that she can come and go as she pleases. Not only does she have a key to my house, she also has a key to my heart.

SEEKING MY EARTHLY FATHER'S APPROVAL

As I grew older, my anger toward my father grew into hatred. Bitterness took root in my heart, and I wanted nothing to do with him—not even when I heard the news that he was about to die.

One day when I was in high school, my sister Deborah told me that my dad was in the hospital with only a short time to live. He had asked me to come visit him so he could make things right. Because of the rage I felt, I told her I wasn't going. She told me she had made peace with him, and she encouraged me to do the same. I still refused.

A couple days later he passed away.

My sister attended the funeral, but I was still so angry that I did not go. In fact, his death intensified my anger. Despite my hardness, though, there was still a part of me that desperately wanted his approval. As the years marched on and I achieved success in business and earned multiple promotions, I often sat in my office and thought about what my father would say about my life. On business trips sitting in boardrooms, making big decisions for corporations, I wondered if he would be proud of me. The inner child in me still yearned for my father's approval, even though I would never receive it.

A conscience-pricking moment came for me in 1997, when I was ordained as a deacon in my church. During the service I remember thinking, "I'm getting ordained to do God's work. And I still hate my father."

FINDING MY HEAVENLY FATHER'S APPROVAL

All the pain and bitterness in my heart came to a head several years later in 2002. I was wrapping up a business trip in Dallas, preparing to fly home to North Carolina, when I missed my flight. I had been a frequent flier for years, and in all that time had never missed a flight. But to avoid foul weather, the plane departed ahead of schedule that day. Little did I know that God orchestrated this for my healing.

With a few hours to spare, I sat down in the terminal and struck up a conversation with a gentleman seated nearby who I found out worked at Dallas Theological Seminary. Our conversation lasted for hours as we shared about our work, our families, and our lives. At one point he paused and asked a simple question that I believe God used to start my healing process: "Joe, why do you work so hard?"

I paused a moment before answering. "Because I want to take care of my family. I want to be the father that I never had."

He smiled. "I'm sure you do. But I don't think that's why you work so hard."

"Sure it is," I replied.

He shook his head. "I know the reason you work so hard: You're trying to please a dead man."

I looked him straight in the eye, feeling a shock wave pulse through my body. "What did you say?" I asked.

"You're trying to please your father, but he's dead. If you want to be the father figure that you desire for your daughter, you must forgive him and move on."

By this time, twenty-two years had passed since my father's passing—years filled with anger, pain, and heaviness of spirit. But now God used the words of a stranger to reach me. Sitting in that Dallas airport, I surrendered to God and admitted how much I hated my father, how weary and tired I was of working to please a dead man. I told Him that if He helped me, I was willing to forgive my father. The healing process began at that moment.

Before I boarded my flight back to North Carolina, I parted ways with my new friend and brother in Christ. I don't remember his name and will probably never meet him again, but if he reads this book, he should know that God used him mightily to help me forgive my father and start living the life He planned for me. I praise God that he used this man as His vessel.

Today, I live a life free of all the resentment, anger, and hatred I harbored for so many years against my father. I have forgiven him. I hope he asked God for forgiveness so that, one day, I can reunite with him in heaven.

THREE LESSONS FOR HEALING

Even as I write this chapter, I feel Satan's attack, because he doesn't want me to share this testimony. He knows the healing and freedom this chapter will bring to those who are reading it. Friend, are you angry over past hurts? Here are three ways to heal.

1. Forgive and Make Peace

Forgiveness is an invaluable gift that we give ourselves. It's easy to think of forgiveness as letting someone else off the hook for what they did. In reality, it provides a channel for our own healing. Once I came to terms with my anger and voluntarily forgave my father that day in the Dallas airport, I instantly felt a sharp pain of regret for not going to the hospital to make peace with my dad before he passed away.

Is there someone in your life you need to forgive? Do it immediately. Now is the time, while that individual is still alive. Don't withhold the opportunity for your healing to take place. I guarantee you that God will free you. It's not too late, but act hastily. Don't wait until you miss your flight like I did.

2. Come to Know Your Heavenly Father

I love watching documentaries about the 1960s and 1970s. Late one night, I had tuned in to a documentary about President John F. Kennedy and the Cuban Missile Crisis. It included a clip of President Kennedy in the Oval Office with his staff, discussing a fundamental strategy concerning the crisis. Although the cameras were on the president and his staff, I couldn't help but notice his son, John Jr., in the corner playing with a toy truck. Several minutes later, a wheel popped off the truck. What did the boy do? To my surprise, he picked up his toy and walked right between the president's security team to jump on his father's lap. Immediately, President Kennedy stopped what he was doing to fix the truck.

I recall thinking to myself, "How can this little boy walk right through the highest level of security and interrupt the most powerful man in the world at this moment?" Then I remembered: "That's John Jr.'s daddy." Sitting there watching the documentary, a wave of sadness swept over me and tears ran down my face. I would never share the same joy of jumping onto my father's lap, of asking him to fix my broken toy. But as only God can do, He allowed the Holy Spirit to visit me with a revelation: "Joe, my son, I know you have never experienced sitting on your earthly father's lap to fix anything for you. But as your heavenly Father, I eagerly desire for you to sit on My lap. Not only will I fix your truck, but I can also fix all your problems, including your broken heart from the absence of your earthly father."

My sadness was instantly overshadowed with the joy that only our heavenly Father can provide!

God is powerful enough to carry your burdens, regardless of the severity of your circumstance. In God's omnipotent and omniscient power, He desires to fill the void that your earthly father cannot fill. He invites all His children to jump on His lap so He can mend our broken hearts. The only security gate we need to get through is confessing and repenting of our sins. Then He will welcome us to jump on his lap.

Isn't it wonderful to know we will never have to cry over our Heavenly father not showing up? He will never leave us.

I once read about a successful man who took his wife and three children with him on a business trip. Before they checked into the hotel, he had to attend a very important meeting, so his family had to go with him and wait outside the boardroom. At one point, the father noticed out of the corner of his eye someone pacing back and forth just beyond the doorway. He realized it was his three-year-old son. When his son passed in full view, the boy slowed down and looked with anticipation toward his dad. The father did not want to make eye contact with his son because he was not sure what his son would do. His son continued walking back and forth, trying to get his father's attention. Finally, this father made eye contact and motioned for his son to come in. There was an immense amount of joy and delight in the boy's face as he smiled, ran into the room, and shouted, "Him wants me! Yes, him wants me!" right in the middle of this important meeting. His father didn't correct the poor use of grammar, instead reaffirming his son with these simple words: "Him wants you."

You may spend your days pacing back and forth, wondering how God feels about you. If so, I have some good news for you: Jesus wants to take you by the hand and lead you to the real you, the person He created you to be. Your view of yourself will change once you see yourself as Jesus does—one who is deeply loved, absolutely forgiven, and forever free. Yes—Him wants you!

3. Fight for Your Family, Not against It

I have a special message for the fathers who are reading this: We are in a fight for our families. We are not in regulation, nor are we in overtime. We are in sudden death. And the struggle is real. It's time that we break the huddle and execute the play that God has given us in protecting our families.

If you do not affirm your children, someone else will. Here's the truly frightening part: It might not be the person you want to affirm them. The first time that our children hear the words "I love you" should come from you. This is especially important for our daughters.

REFLECTION

Dads, how has God made you a better father? Below, share your thoughts with God about how you can be a better father. Is there someone you need to forgive, or someone you need to seek forgiveness from? Write it down and ask God to guide you to victory.

_____

_____

_____

_____

_____

_____

_____

_____

_____

_____

_____

_____

_____

_____

_____

_____

_____

_____

_____

_____

_____

CHAPTER # 4
A COACH'S LOVE AND HOW GOD USED FOOTBALL TO SHAPE MY LIFE

When I started playing football in middle school, building character and learning life lessons were not on my mind. I was thinking about scoring points and winning games! And that is exactly what my team did. We only lost one game the two seasons I played. Our winning streak ended, though, when my teammates and I started high school. Sophomore year, our junior varsity team lost all 10 games of the regular season.

This topple—from champions to losers—was embarrassing and discouraging. Clearly, our team lacked leadership and discipline; we lost winnable games because of those deficits. We were also prideful and overly confident, believing that our success in middle school exempted us from the need to adapt and grow to compete on the high school level.

Winning is impossible when you don't execute and play as a team!

Thankfully, a man showed up who gave us the leadership and discipline we needed: Coach Bruce Peterson.

I met Coach Peterson during summer workouts as a rising

junior. It was anything but comfortable. Coach's message was clear: If we prepared and played together as a team, we had a great shot at winning *all* of our games. I scratched my head, wondering if he knew that our JV team lost *every* game that past season. And the varsity team we were joining was coming off a losing season, too. Tensions were high—the younger players were not mixing well with the older ones. We were more like rivals than teammates.

Coach Peterson made it clear that we had the talent to win, but it was up to us to come together as a team. We had to leave our egos at the door. We had to show up for each other.

Our team captain, Robert Fields (an amazing football player), echoed Coach's words when he said, "Let's come together and put all our energy into challenging each other and preparing like thoroughbreds."

With this inspiration and encouragement motivating us, our team worked hard all summer. Two-a-days (back-to-back workouts in one day) were especially intense and gave us an opportunity to step it up and demand even more of ourselves. By fall, our team was exactly what Coach Peterson envisioned. We went undefeated and won our Western 4A Conference championship. In one year we went from the bottom to the top!

Looking back, I can see the way playing football prepared me for the challenges of adulthood. God used it to teach me virtue, teamwork, and self-sacrifice.

MY SUBSTITUTE DAD

I grew close to Coach Peterson during my senior year. His leadership skills were unmatched. He prepared his players to win games and championships, but that's not what made him a true standout. He didn't just coach us to win at football, he coached us to win at life. Coach taught us how to be men and take responsibility for our actions and attitudes. He taught us to own up to whatever we did, whether good or bad. He cared about every one of us, and I noticed that.

I wanted Coach Peterson to be proud of me, so I played hard for him. Even more than winning for myself, I wanted to win for him.

I'll always remember the day Coach Peterson walked over to me after a game, took me by the shoulders, and said he was proud of me and he loved me. What an emotional moment! I fought back tears because I didn't want my teammates to see me cry. His outreach came at a key time in my life. I did not have a father in the stands cheering for me, but I had a coach who cheered me on and parented me at the same time.

Why would a white man tell a black boy from the projects he loved him? I could not fathom it. That man brought racial healing and unity to our team. I played for him in the early 1980s, when racism was still rampant where I lived. It was unheard of for black and white boys from diverse backgrounds to say they loved each other and to protect each other as brothers. Our coach's insistence on us executing as a team made the difference. He taught us how to love each other so well. As a coach, he prepared his team for every season and every game.

I am thankful that Coach Peterson loved me despite our different skin colors. His example influenced the way I treat people and taught me how to fight through pain to achieve my goals in life. I believe God used Coach Peterson to do the same for many of his players. The hard work and commitment we learned from him earned our team another Western 4A Conference championship my senior year. But the foundation Coach Peterson put underneath us has the power to endure for a lifetime.

Decades later, my high school team is still a brand of brothers. One day, years ago, my daughter, Danielle, overheard me chatting on the phone with my childhood friend, Jonathan Crooks. I've known Jonathan since first grade, and we played football together. He was a teammate who challenged me during summers to stay in shape and push till I was beyond tired. Before we hung up the phone, I told him I loved him. My daughter, puzzled, asked me why. "Because he's my brother," I replied.

Coach Peterson taught us that there are three types of people in the world:

- People who *watch* what happens;
- People who *wonder* what happens; and
- People who *make* things happen

He told us it was up to us to decide which type of person we wanted to be. And he was a firsthand example to us of someone who makes things happen. This wisdom has helped me during tumultuous times. I've chosen to follow my coach's lead and stay in the group that makes things happen.

MAKING THE TOUCHDOWN THAT REALLY MATTERS

A few years ago I visited Coach Peterson in the hospital. He told me he might die. We discussed his medical condition briefly before shifting the conversation to a trip down memory lane. He remembered how much I loved to run one of our plays called the "48-sweep." I was a linebacker and the leading blocker, directing many running backs into the end zone to score touchdowns with that play. We agreed that the 48-sweep was our bread-and-butter play. When all else failed, we could always go back to that play.

Once our conversation slowed, Coach looked over to me and said, "Joe, I want to live, and I am going to do everything possible to fight for my life. I have no regrets and I've always tried to do the right thing."

Fighting back tears, I told Coach how much he meant to me and that I loved him. I thanked him for loving me. Then I told him I wanted to run the 48-sweep one more time for him, not to lead a running back into the end zone, but to lead *him* into the end zone. I explained that heaven is the ultimate end zone. I asked him if he had accepted Christ as his Savior. That touchdown determines where we spend eternity. Coach looked at me and said, "Joe, I have accepted Christ as my Savior, and if I die, I believe I will go to heaven."

Before I left the hospital, I asked coach if I could pray for him, and he agreed. As we prayed, we cried tears of hope and love. After we finished, Coach reassured me he was going to fight to live, and that if the good Lord planned to take him, He would have a whistle ready for him in heaven. I'm thankful to report that our gracious heavenly Father healed Coach, and he is still living a quality life today.

Love you, coach!

REFLECTION

Share your thoughts below about how someone in your life has influenced and encouraged you. Call them today and thank them. No texting—they need to hear your voice speak those words!

_____

_____

_____

_____

_____

_____

_____

_____

_____

_____

_____

_____

_____

_____

_____

_____

_____

_____

_____

_____

CHAPTER # 5
I AM A MAN, NOW WHAT?

My senior year of high school, several colleges contacted me about football scholarships. I was disappointed to hear that none of them wanted to use me as a linebacker, the position I loved playing. Instead, the college coaches talked to me about playing cornerback or safety or fullback. I didn't have peace about any of those positions, so I made the tough decision not to continue any conversations with those colleges. While many of my friends went off to college, I chose a different path. I jumped into the workforce and took college courses at night.

My transition to adulthood was bumpy. With most of my friends at college, I was lonely. Going to my high school stadium to watch Friday night games was a letdown. When fans told me how much they enjoyed watching me play in the past, it left me empty. I felt a major void, knowing I had to face the fact I would probably never play football again, a game I loved and that taught me so much.

To compensate for my loss, I focused on work. I started as an hourly employee at an automotive company. My first few assignments included sweeping, loading trucks, and shoveling snow off the driveway during the winter. I wasn't afraid of hard work—my typical workday comprised moving heavy equipment like carburetors and engines—and it paid off. It wasn't too long before my boss promoted me to receiving clerk and, later, put me in the management-training program.

After finishing the management program, I joined an elite group of troubleshooters sent to various locations throughout the country to help with mergers and acquisitions. Soon I became a manager based in Columbia, SC. After that, another promotion took me to Memphis, TN. Finally, I ended up in the corporate office in Raleigh, NC.

FINDING MY WIFE

As I climbed the corporate ladder, each decision to move carried extra weight because I was dating Janet, a beautiful young woman in my hometown. I felt torn about moving because it meant leaving her and my mother behind. But they both gave me their blessing and encouraged me to take the promotions. I continued to do well at work, but it was a struggle to be apart from the women I loved.

My dilemma ended when Janet and I got married in 1987. Thirty-four years later, we are still going strong!

Before I started dating Janet, I prayed for a year that God would lead me to a godly and beautiful wife. He answered those prayers beyond my expectations. Janet is a godly woman, and she is amazingly beautiful both inside and out.

It has taken me many years to comprehend what a precious gift from God Janet is to me. My goal is to be a great steward over what He has entrusted to me and to love her as Christ loves the church. It is my joy to protect, care for, and honor her as my wife.

Janet's value to our family is incalculable. Whenever she's not feeling up to par, my daughter and I hold the house down the best we can. Things do not go well for us! The little things that Janet does to make our house a home can't be replicated by anyone else. I know that I have found favor with the Lord through my wife's character, prayers, and relationship with God.

There is no doubt when God inspired Solomon to write this passage, He had Janet in mind for me:

He who finds a wife finds what is good and receives favor from the Lord. (Proverbs 18:22)

Husbands, this passage is so full of truth:

Husbands, in the same way be considerate as you live with your wives, and treat them with respect as the weaker partner and heirs with you of the gracious gift of life, so that nothing will hinder your prayers. (1 Peter 3:7)

I wish I had known how crucial this counsel was before I got married, but God has been faithful to teach me how to be the husband He created me to be. When both a husband and a wife make up their minds to surrender fully to God, He can correct every mistake and guide them through every challenge.

LEARNING TO BE A HUSBAND AND FATHER

For many couples the first years of marriage are a major transition. Husbands and wives must learn to cooperate and face challenges together. Janet and I faced significant lifestyle changes. While I was adjusting to the increasing demands of my job and a relocation, Janet moved from Asheville, NC, to Columbia, SC, and just four months later moved again—this time to Memphis, TN. We also welcomed our baby girl, Danielle, into the world in Memphis.

Both of our mothers came from Asheville to help us when Danielle was born, but once they left the pressures of work and home were intense and often isolating. We desperately missed our families, who lived ten hours away by car. Memphis had a high crime rate and many unsafe areas, so it was a difficult place to get involved with a healthy community. One thing Janet enjoyed was going to Target. She took Danielle there so often that, to this day, it's her favorite store!

We needed emotional, spiritual, and financial support but felt we had no place to go and no one to turn to. More than once I thought about quitting my job and moving my family back home to Asheville. But I knew one thing for sure: failure was not an option for us.

Sometimes it felt like we could never get ahead. Even so, Janet rarely complained. She supported me working strenuous hours.

She encouraged me to take more promotions, and that meant more relocations. We were intent on improving our lives. As I took on bigger roles, my travel schedule became more demanding. But whenever I returned from a business trip, Janet always greeted me with a kiss and a warm hug. What a special blessing after traveling—often times returning from another country.

My wife and I were a real team. It elated me to know I had her love and support as we depended on each other to get through hard times.

A wife of noble character who can find? She is worth far more than rubies. Her husband has full confidence in her and lacks nothing of value. She brings him good, not harm all the days of her life. (Proverbs 31:11-12)

Janet is a smart lady. She could have chosen any career she wanted, and she decided to raise our daughter at home and support my career, believing it was the best role for her and offered the greatest payoff for our family. Janet has made our home a peaceful, beautiful, and safe place. Danielle and I can't thank her enough and will always be grateful for her sacrifices.

I know there were times Janet must have felt she was taking on more than she could bear, but through it all she stayed positive and persevered. Although I have done my best to be a godly father, I give Janet credit for being the parent who has demonstrated a level of selflessness that makes her Danielle's finest example. She is so blessed to have Janet as her mother (the best in the world)!

Her children arise and call her blessed; her husband also, and he praises her. Many women do noble things, but you surpass them all. Charm is deceptive, and beauty is fleeting; but a woman who fears the Lord is to be praised. (Proverbs 31:28–30)

Danielle is a beautiful daughter and the apple of my eye. Janet and I are so proud of her. She is the perfect daughter! Of all the titles I have achieved through life, there is none more honorable than "father." Danielle is tender like Janet yet tough like me. She loves God with an uncompromising commitment to His Word. Knowing that Danielle has accepted Jesus as her Lord and Savior is more important to me than any accolade I could ever receive!

I humbly thank God for my beautiful family!

REFLECTION

What burdens do you carry as a spouse, a parent, a son, or a daughter? Write them down. Then, place your burdens at the feet of God the Potter, who knows how to shape you into what He would have you be.

_____

_____

_____

_____

_____

_____

_____

_____

_____

_____

_____

_____

_____

_____

_____

_____

_____

_____

_____

_____

CHAPTER # 6
FROM THE PROJECTS
TO THE BOARDROOM

As a boy I dreamed of escaping the projects and finding a job that paid $50,000 a year. I thought I was dreaming big! But God's plans for me were greater than I ever imagined. Only He could take a young black boy from the projects and set him in boardrooms around the world as a corporate leader.

I've conducted meetings in places like New York, California, Canada, Mexico, and Europe, and I was often the only person in the room who didn't have an Ivy League degree. People with professional degrees and doctorates reported to me, yet I did not graduate from college. Only God's favor explains why that was possible.

I have witnessed the truth in these verses firsthand:

Commit to the Lord whatever you do, and your plans will succeed. (Proverbs 16:3)

Jesus replied, "What is impossible with men is possible with God." (Luke 18:27)

Before I go on, it is important to clarify that I enthusiastically support higher education and do not minimize its importance. I invested more than $100,000 in my daughter's college degree and encourage everyone to go to college or learn a trade after high school. As Franz Kafka said, "Better to have, and not need, than to need, and not have."

However, God's will is more important to me than anything else. Although I took classes and have several certifications, His plan for my life did not require me to get a full degree. I'm grateful for investments some of my employers made to provide me with the best executive education at top institutions. I completed advance management programs in global supply chain strategy and management at Massachusetts Institute of Technology (MIT) Sloan School of Management, customer relations management at the University of Wisconsin-Madison School of Business, and executive leadership training at the Center for Creative Leadership in Greensboro, NC. God led me along the trajectory He ordained for my career, and I'm satisfied with His sovereignty over my life.

RISING THROUGH THE RANKS

My lack of a traditional education posed challenges at times, particularly when I was meeting a group of principals, board members, and senior-level executives of a corporation for the first time when invited to help lead a merger and acquisition. During lunch breaks in the boardrooms, my colleagues and I often enjoyed chatting and getting to know one another. The conversations often turned to alma maters, where some had earned not only an undergraduate degree, but often MBAs, master's degrees, or doctorates. Those moments were always uncomfortable for me. It was tough explaining that I rose through the ranks the hard way: working while attending night school, accepting several promotions, and ending up in a high-level position that left no time to complete my degree.

I initially felt ashamed because many of my colleagues had spent a decade or more in postsecondary education, yet I was the person leading the meetings and, in most cases, making final decisions. Eventually, though, my shame gave way to humility and gratitude. Nothing but God's favor can explain my success. He enabled me to work hard, and He opened doors at the right time.

The one that calls you is faithful, and he will do it. (1 Thessalonians 5:24)

God's grace helped me maintain confidence when self-doubt could have derailed me. I've received plenty of rejection throughout my career, but I've learned that God will have His way regardless of whether everyone likes me or wants to work with me. I've been promoted by people who didn't like me and didn't understand why they were promoting me!

When a man's plans are pleasing to the Lord, he makes even his enemies live at peace with him. (Proverbs 16:7)

In times of struggle, I reminded myself that God has His hand on my life. He is going to accomplish His will in my life whether or not I have a degree. When I prayed, God reminded me it was His power, not mine, accomplishing these things. He was demonstrating His power. God's Word assured me that when He appoints you, He anoints you.

I often went back to these verses in times of doubt:

Now to Him who is able to do exceeding abundantly above all that we ask or think, according to the power that works in us. (Ephesians 3:20)

In his heart a man plans his course, but the Lord determines his steps. (Proverbs 16:9)

MBA REQUIRED, BUT GOD HAD OTHER PLANS

With God in the lead, my career has taken a few unconventional turns. Years ago He pressed me to apply for a role that required an MBA. I submitted my application and received an invitation to interview. A highly credentialed panel of professionals interviewed me, assuming I had an MBA. No one asked me about my education until the closing minutes of the interview. They were shocked to learn I didn't have an undergraduate degree, much less an MBA.

"Do you know this position requires an MBA?" the president of the company asked me, clearly annoyed.

"I do," I replied.

"Then why did you apply if you knew the qualifications beforehand?"

I took a deep breath, looked him straight in the eye, and replied, "Sir, during this interview process I've heard everyone on the panel share that the current and previous people in this position both had MBAs. But they didn't lead this company to your satisfaction. I have a track record that shows I *can* do this job. I will not only meet your expectations, I will exceed them."

"We understand," replied the president, "but an MBA is still part of the job requirement."

Everyone closed their notebooks. The interview had been going on for two hours, but everyone stopped listening after they learned that I lacked a key qualification.

"May I ask one last question?" I asked before the meeting officially ended.

The president nodded.

"Was I a serious candidate for this position before you learned that I don't have an MBA, and did you feel confident that I could do the job?"

I told them they didn't have to give me an answer on the spot. I kindly thanked them for their time and excused myself from the room.

Two days later the president called me. "Joe, I can't believe I'm calling you, but after some discussion we want to hire you for the position," he said. "Our only requirement is that you meet with one of our principals and the board members of the company first."

As I listened to him, I whispered to myself, "Yes, God, You are the man!" I thanked the president and the next day met with the company officials. The following day I received a formal offer.

A man's gift opens doors for him and brings him before great men. (Proverbs 18:16)

When God's blessings are on your life, there is nothing anybody can do to stop them. I worked at that company for fifteen years, received five promotions, and oversaw the entire North American operation, which included several facilities in the United States and Canada. I work hard and am fully dedicated to my roles, but I know without a doubt that the original source of my success is God's incomparable grace!

[2] *The Lord was with Joseph so that he prospered, and he lived in the house of his Egyptian master.* [3] *When his master saw that the Lord was with him and that the Lord gave him success in everything he did,* [4] *Joseph found favor in his eyes and became his attendant. Potiphar put him in charge of his household, and he entrusted to his care everything he owned.*

I feel a special connection to God when I read the verses above. To experience Him being with me in so many situations through the years and granting me such favor does not make sense to my human eye. I must look through my spiritual eye to understand the relationship I have with the Lord. I can only imagine how Joseph felt knowing that God was with him. I know one thing for sure—the Lord has been with this Joseph every moment of my life!

REFLECTION

Think of ways that God has shown you favor. List them below and thank Him for His blessings.

_____

_____

_____

_____

_____

_____

_____

_____

_____

_____

_____

_____

_____

_____

_____

_____

_____

_____

_____

_____

_____

_____

CHAPTER # 7
A NEW CALL ON MY LIFE

What does success truly mean? How do you know when you've achieved it?

In my twenties and thirties, my primary goal was to become a successful business executive. I craved accomplishment and ran hard after my boyhood dreams. God blessed me and allowed me to build a strong and successful career. But no matter how many promotions I received, a hollowness lurked inside me that I did not understand. The thoughts kept circulating through my mind: "I have a beautiful wife and a wonderful daughter, am at the top of my career and am making more money than I ever expected. I've earned accolades for my achievements, leadership, and results."

So why didn't I have peace and fulfillment?

GOD ALTERED MY DEFINITION OF SUCCESS

Flying back from a European business trip years ago, I took time to reflect on God's amazing mercy for my family and me. I was forty-one. Influencing peopling all over the world and providing the best for my family were things I did not take for granted. Tears of joy rolled down my face as I recalled how far God had brought me, *a little boy from the projects raised by a single mother was now traveling all over the world and making major decisions for corporations*. I praised Him for the many blessings He gave me. Certainly, I had thanked God many times before, but I experienced something different that day.

My moments of praise turned to somber reflection when I heard the voice of God share these words: "Joe, it's not good enough *ANYMORE* for you to celebrate your *BLESSINGS*, to sit around thinking about how good I have been to *YOU*, when there are thousands of people who need you to walk beside them so that I can show them My mercy through you. I am calling you to love and mentor them. They need to know that I love them, and just as I have made a way for you, I will make a way for them."

The Holy Spirit spoke to my heart strongly, "Son, to whom much is given, much is required."

"God, can I have this moment to *just* give you praise for the things you have done for me?" I asked.

His voice clearly replied, "Stop using excuses and do what I have commanded you to do." God said He will judge me on what I do with the gifts He gave me. There is a final exam waiting for me on judgment day.

Let me be clear: born-again Christians receive eternal life through the grace God gives us. But salvation is only the first step in pleasing our Father. As followers of Jesus Christ, we will one day give an account for the choices we make.

For as the body without the spirit is dead, so faith without works is dead also. (James 2:26)

As I evaluated my life, I saw what needed to change. Immediately I decided to obey the Lord. More than anything else, I want to hear God say on that day of reckoning, "Well done, good and faithful servant."

I heard the voice of God telling me, "My son, you must redefine what success truly means." He was absolutely right. I needed to let go of my self-centered perspective so that I could see success the way God does. John Maxwell describes it so well: *"Success is when I add value to myself. Significance is when I add value to others."*

Sitting there on the plane, I made a bargain with the Lord. I told Him I would open his Word to hear more from Him, hoping to read something encouraging. Because of the strong conviction I felt, something like the story of Jesus healing a paralyzed or blind man or calming a storm would have been welcome. Motivation and excitement were what I sought. But guess what I turned to? Matthew 25:31–46, where Jesus talks about the final exam.

When the Son of Man comes in his glory, and all the angels with him, he will sit on his glorious throne. All the nations will be gathered before him, and he will separate the people one from another as a shepherd separates the sheep from the goats. He will put the sheep on his right and the goats on his left. Then the King will say to those on his right, "Come, you who are blessed by my Father; take your inheritance, the kingdom prepared for you since the creation of the world. For I was hungry, and you gave me something to eat, I was thirsty and you gave me something to drink, I was a stranger and you invited me in, I needed clothes and you clothed me, I was sick and you looked after me, I was in prison and you came to visit me."

Then the righteous will answer him, "Lord, when did we see you hungry and feed you, or thirsty and give you something to drink? When did we see you a stranger and invite you in, or needing clothes and clothe you? When did we see you sick or in prison and go to visit you?"

The King will reply, "Truly I tell you, whatever you did for one of the least of these brothers and sisters of mine, you did for me."

Then he will say to those on his left, "Depart from me, you who are cursed, into the eternal fire prepared for the devil and his angels. For I was hungry, and you gave me nothing to eat, I was thirsty, and you gave me nothing to drink, I was a stranger and you did not invite me in, I needed clothes and you did not clothe me, I was sick and in prison and you did not look after me."

They also will answer, "Lord, when did we see you hungry or thirsty or a stranger or needing clothes or sick or in prison, and did not help you?"

He will reply, "Truly I tell you, whatever you did not do for one of the least of these, you did not do for me." Then they will go away to eternal punishment, but the righteous to eternal life.

I knew God wanted to fix my attention on His purpose for me. I realized reading those Scriptures that God was allowing me to take an open-book test. He wants to ensure I am fully prepared for my final exam. I thought about what my exam will be like when I come face-to-face with God. A few things came to my mind.

God will not ask me:

- How much money I made,
- What neighborhood I lived in,
- What type of car I drove, or
- How many promotions I received.

God already knows about these things because He blessed and entrusted me with *His money*, *His houses*, *His cars*, and all the success I had achieved.

The Bible clearly spells out what questions will be on my final exam:

- Did you visit Me when I was sick?
- Did you give Me water when I was thirsty?
- Did you feed Me when I was hungry?
- Did you clothe Me when I was naked?
- Did you visit Me when I was in prison?

As I processed all of this I tried to find a way out of fully committing to my assignment. We can be very creative when we don't want to do something!

I asked: "God, how could You ever be sick, when You not only healed the sick but raised up the dead to walk again? Lord, how could You ever be thirsty, when the very first miracle You performed was changing water into wine? And by the way, You said it was excellent wine! How could You ever be hungry, Lord? You could have turned the rock into a steak if you wanted. It is impossible for You to be hungry. Lord, how could You be naked when Your Father, the Father of all creation, clothed Adam and Eve? Surely, He would have clothed His Son. Lord, how could You be locked in prison, when in Your Word there are many times when You unlocked prison cells for Your people?"

Trying to challenge God didn't work for me. It won't work for you, either.

As clearly as God spoke to me that day, I'm sad to say I didn't fully embrace the message. Even after feeling God's presence so strongly, once the plane landed and I was no longer forty thousand feet above the Atlantic Ocean, I went back to business as usual. I acted a lot like Jonah did when God gave him an assignment to go to Nineveh and tell the citizens of that city to repent.

The word of the Lord came to Jonah, son of Amittai: "Go to the great city of Nineveh and preach against it, because its wickedness has come up before me." But Jonah ran away from the Lord and headed for Tarshish. He went down to Joppa, where he found a ship bound for that port. After paying the fare, he went aboard and sailed for Tarshish to flee from the Lord. Then the Lord sent a great wind on the sea, and such a violent storm arose the ship threatened to break up. (Jonah 1:1–4)

I am eternally grateful that God kept working with me as He did with Jonah (read the entire book of Jonah to see how the story ended). He is a creative and persuasive Father who corrects us out of love, but the best time to say yes to God is the first time He asks.

REFLECTION

Has God redirected your path at key moments in your life? How did you react? Are you where He wants you to be right now?

_____

_____

_____

_____

_____

_____

_____

_____

_____

_____

_____

_____

_____

_____

_____

_____

_____

_____

_____

_____

_____

CHAPTER # 8
A DARK SEASON

God allowed a dark shadow of anxiety to descend upon me in 2006. Prior to this dark season God gave me many warnings to accept my calling.

It all started when my daughter, Danielle, started having major headaches during her freshman year in college. The headaches were so severe she began to think she had brain cancer. Her physical and mental turmoil weighed heavily on me. After months of testing, multiple trips to doctor, and several trips to the emergency room, we still had no answers what was causing her headaches. One night, my wife noticed that Danielle's headaches would start after she eat. My wife looked in Danielle's mouth with a flashlight and saw more teeth than she could count! We had found the cause of her pain: her wisdom teeth. Once her wisdom teeth were removed, she had no more problems. It was pure relief. Looking back, I believe God used this situation to get my attention because of the affect it had on me.

God was still getting my attention. My mom became sick and Janet's back went out. The way each of these situations affected me, I look back and believe God was trying to get my attention.

If all of this was not enough, there was a rainy Saturday morning that I won't forget. I went for a drive that Saturday morning with no intention to test drive a new car, especially not a Volvo! However, I found myself at a dealership. The dealership was just opening, and the salesperson allowed me to take the car out on a test drive by myself. As I was turning back into the dealership at the end of the test drive, the rain had not let up. Because of the rain, another car couldn't stop and hit the car that I was test driving.

I can remember getting out of the car, standing in the rain, and hearing God's voice asking, "When you are going to get it?" The car was totaled, but I didn't even have a scratch on my body. In fact, when the police arrived, the officer asked if the ambulance had already taken the people that was in the car I was driving. When the officer realized that I was the one driving the car, he could not believe it. Only God knew to have me test drive the safest car built to try and get my attention.

That morning at the dealership seemed to come out of nowhere and it began to affect every area of my life. I was at the top of my career, but I now found myself facing a new challenge with anxiety. I was bewildered that I went from facilitating long board meetings all over the country, to being unable to sit in a meeting for more than five minutes at a time. I normally felt in control, but now life seemed utterly unruly.

Seeking relief, I took a week off work. When I returned, I could only handle working half days for the next several weeks. One Saturday morning I drove to work, hoping to catch up, only to pass through the parking lot and go back home. I wondered if I'd ever be able to board a plane again. The thought of flying terrified me. How could I do my job if I couldn't fly?

In order for me to sleep, my wife rubbed my back every night the same way you would rub a baby's back. I knew I couldn't live this way indefinitely. How could I continue to support my family if I was this debilitated?

I gradually realized I was never in control of my life the way I thought I was.

After deciding to see a Christian counselor, I asked him this question: "Larry, do you think I will ever be the same again?"

"Joe, you won't be the same again," he answered.

I sat in silence for a few seconds (which felt like a lifetime). Larry continued, "Now that God has your attention, you will be better than you have ever been."

As those words sunk in, I could almost hear the theme song from Rocky playing in the background. I was ready to fight! When someone loses their confidence and hope, a word of encouragement has the power to put them back on track.

When a dark season descends, it is very important to understand clearly why it appears. Failing to understand can mean failing to escape that dark place. If you recover but continue to disobey God, He may allow another trial in your life until you choose to surrender to His will.

God allowed a dark season in my life, but not because He doesn't love me. He allowed it because He does love me and wants to use me for His glory. God wanted to get my attention so I can fulfill the purpose He has ordained for my life. I disobeyed Him and refused to acknowledge my call to speak His Word. His plan was not in line with my agenda or my idea of success, so He acted out of mercy and grace to persuade me to see things His way. I am grateful to have a heavenly Father who corrects His children.

I asked God to restore my peace if I committed to pursue His will for my life. He granted my plea. Peace is priceless. It's not something we can buy on Amazon with Prime delivery. We must go to God if we want true peace, for He is the one who controls the supply. How can we risk giving up our peace by not doing what He asks of us?

After my anxiety lifted, Janet and I developed a plan for me to leave my job. I was forty-three when the dark season began. We planned for me to transition out of my job by age fifty-five. During this time, God opened many doors for me to share His Word and encourage other people: I spoke at my church and other local churches, at men's conferences, and I spoke at CEO luncheons, the YMCA, high-school football pre-games, and prisons.

However, I was still not "all in" on the transition from my career to my purpose . . .

MORE WARNING SIGNS

Note: I avoided writing this section for over a year. I feared that revisiting painful memories would take me back to a dark place. But my editor encouraged me to move forward prayerfully, because it is an important part of my story. I have considered not writing this section more times than I can remember. However, I trusted God to protect me as I went back to an uncomfortable place so that I can help others avoid some of my mistakes. As you read these words, you will soon discover why I put off writing them.

I turned fifty-two in 2015. Our family went to the beach and spent some much-needed quality time together. Early each morning I had quiet time with God while watching the beautiful ocean. It was medicine to my soul. The Lord spoke to my heart about leaving my company before I turned fifty-five, which was several years sooner than Janet and I had planned. I knew God wanted me to follow through.

After we returned from vacation, I met with the president of my company and the director of human resources to discuss leaving the organization. I offered to stay and work on an extended notice to help recruit and train my replacement. The company responded by giving me a salary increase and an equity salary adjustment with a new executive compensation package. My earnings rose to a level I had never dreamed possible. Once again, I delayed doing what the Lord asked of me. ***The money made it much harder to walk away.***

A year later, I had no drive. I was unhappy. I had a posh office and was running the North American operations, which was the largest operations within the company, and *yet my peace had disappeared again.*

I remember walking by my office one day and seeing my name and title on the door. I thought, "*I'm successful at the wrong things. I'm at the top of the ladder yet feel nothing but emptiness as I look down from this high perch all alone.*" Feeling sick, I left my office for an early lunch. I did nothing but drive around and wonder what was wrong with me. *I was more financially secure than at any time in my life, but it felt like I was living in worse poverty than I did as a boy in the projects. I was spiritually bankrupt because I was not obeying God by pursuing my purpose.*

BURNED OUT

In 2016 several of my long-time friends passed away. Months later, a man who was a mentor and father figure to me died. I grieved deeply for those men, and it took a lot out of me. I noticed it was getting difficult to do things as simple as get a haircut without feeling anxiety. In the barber's chair I felt so dizzy I thought I would fall to the floor. Even picking up a few items at the grocery store made me anxious. Standing in line was like having a tooth pulled. It was hard to go out to dinner with my family and enjoy our time together. I had trouble sitting through church services on Sundays. I often left the pew early and waited for my family in the car.

One Sunday I was scheduled to speak at church, and it was a battle just getting to the building. But once I started speaking, the anxiety fell away. *Speaking God's Word and sharing with others were the few moments that gave me peace.*

One morning in early 2017, I began walking down a hallway at work and felt like I was going to fall over. A couple of colleagues took me to the emergency room. The hospital staff ran several tests, did lab work, and gave me a full examination. The doctor said he found nothing physically wrong and believed I was experiencing anxiety, but I strongly disagreed with him. I vividly remembered my dark season of anxiety in 2006 and would not believe that I was back in that place. After going back to work, I tried to forget what had happened.

My annual physical was in April. My doctor listed issues I needed to address if I wanted to avoid serious health challenges. Nevertheless, I resolved to work until I was fifty-five and did not plan to follow his advice.

After months of not feeling like myself, I met with the president of my company again in October. I let him know I intended to leave at the end of 2018. This time he did not try to dissuade me; he knew my heart. Inside of me, though, things were far less settled. I kept thinking of ways to continue working beyond age fifty-five. If I was careful to take plenty of time to rest and relax, I thought I would be okay. But every time I started down the wrong path, God was there to correct my course.

Janet and Danielle pointed out that I was less fun and more serious than normal. They also noticed that I was taking muscle relaxers just to calm down and go to sleep. They both asked to me leave my job so I could take time off to rest. I did not heed their advice.

A few months later, driving home from work one evening in March 2018, I felt stressed beyond measure. *I kept thinking, "If I don't leave my job, I'm going to have a heart attack, a stroke, or a nervous breakdown."* None of those options sounded good! It was hard to sleep. I felt like a heavyweight champion who was still fighting after he should have retired. I could keep my hands up but didn't have enough strength to punch back.

On Friday, April 13, 2018, I called my wife in the early afternoon and told her I left my office and was driving around so I could calm down. I let her know I was ready to resign the next Monday. After that, I called one of my mentors and got his wise counsel.

Sunday, April 15, I turned fifty-five. On Monday, April 16, I submitted my formal resignation. After completing my notice, I departed in May. I was in a place I had not been in for over thirty-six years—not working.

My family went on a vacation to get away and give me some time to rest. One evening while we were relaxing, I mentioned to Janet that I planned to take thirty days off to rest. She said I needed at least three months off to recover, but I couldn't imagine taking that much time off. After vacation I had lunch with my pastor, and he counseled me to take six months off. He could see, like Janet, that I was burned out. I couldn't see it.

As the days and weeks went by, though, my body started decompressing. I stopped numbing myself to get through the day. That's when I finally saw that *I was burned out*. My wife and my pastor were right. I scheduled a visit with my doctor because I wasn't feeling well. He explained to me that ***being under severe stress for a long period of time often causes anxiety***. He confirmed, as Janet and my pastor did, that I needed more time off than I anticipated.

As other companies heard the news of me leaving my job, I started getting calls from them. None of those conversations got off the ground because my tank was completely empty. My passion for leading a corporation was gone.

God finally had me where He wanted me!

What began as thirty days off stretched into the three months Janet recommended. Then three months stretched into the six months my pastor prescribed. I didn't work or do much at all. After a year off, I felt guilty for not working. I didn't know how to rest. Janet assured me I had taken wonderful care of our family and that I had earned the right to rest, but I felt like a loser. Even so, I was too depleted to pick myself up and get anything done. Some days I drove for hours, wondering if I'd ever get my strength and energy back.

Gradually, I turned to the Lord more and more. My fellowship with Him had a major upswing. Instead of viewing time with the Lord as another task on my checklist, it became the best part of my day.

I continued having dizzy spells. Janet often brought my dinner to the family room because I couldn't sit at the dinner table. In June 2019 I was so dizzy I couldn't stand up, so we went to the ER. I was admitted and taken by ambulance to the hospital. With all the machines hooked up to me, I was frightened and bewildered. What was wrong? I'd never been in an ambulance or admitted to a hospital. The staff ran tests and kept me overnight. The next morning I was discharged because all the tests came back negative. I was sent home with a heart monitor for twenty-one days, but nothing of concern showed up.

The doctors couldn't find anything physically wrong with me. My problem was spiritual.

Janet's faith stayed steady, and she kept encouraging me, but I could see that she was concerned. She encouraged me to go on a retreat at the Billy Graham Training Center at The Cove in Asheville.

I did not want to go, so she reminded me I could also visit my mom while I was in Asheville. That was all I needed to hear. *Thank God for my wife. She knows how to motivate me.* Pastor Darren Thomas did a three-day retreat on Psalm 23. One night he spoke on verse 3 of the psalm:

He restores my soul: he leads me in the paths of righteousness for His name's sake.

Pastor Thomas broke down the Scriptures like I have never heard before, and it truly blessed me. *God knew my soul needed to be restored!*

The Sunday morning before the retreat ended, I sat alone in the chapel with tears sliding down my face. **I had an honest conversation with God, confessing I trusted Him but needed my peace and strength back before I could fulfill my purpose.** I was still not completely healed from my burnout. The process was taking so much longer than I expected because what needed to be set right was deep within my soul. Impatience is one of my tendencies; I wanted God to wave His hand and heal me so I could move on. God is much more patient, especially when it comes to healing His children inwardly.

God was willing to wait until I was solidly in line with His plan for me. I was still hanging on to my experiences when I needed to lean fully on Him and depend on Him.

THANK GOD FOR GOOD FRIENDS

Faithful are the wounds of a friend; but the kisses of an enemy are deceitful. (Proverbs 27:8)

After the retreat, I met with some godly men in the marketing business to get advice on branding the new company I was developing. I had started working on it before leaving my job and initially named it 3C Ministries. To avoid confusing potential customers, they suggested I remove my past experiences from my website and LinkedIn profile and focus only on 3C. But I was not ready to let go because it meant letting go of the way I had provided for my family for thirty-six years.

Unfortunately, I still doubted God's ability to provide.

Companies weren't reaching out to me as they had shortly after I left my job, so I decided to send my resume to some organizations I was interested in. I expected to hear back right away but got no responses. I wasn't hearing much from executive recruiters either.

In the past, they contacted me frequently about meeting with their clients to discuss senior leadership roles. Those calls and emails had stopped. I grew frustrated. I called my friend Keith Conely, whom I've known for over thirty years and who was best man at my wedding, to get his opinion. He listened as I shared my aggravation.

Keith responded, "***What you are doing, Humphries?*** I thought we agreed you would not send any more resumes out and would trust God to open doors for you so you can fulfill your purpose. If you believe God took you out of corporate America, why are you trying to go back? If God wanted you to get another job, you would have already gotten at least one offer and maybe more."

My friend's words got my attention because he is one of the nicest guys I know. But he wasn't so nice that day!

I didn't listen to Keith and ended up having a few conversations with some recruiters. I let them know that I wanted to find another job *and* not pursue my purpose. God did not miss a beat, though. After several chats, one of recruiters asked, "Why are you searching for a corporate job when you need to be telling your story to bless people?"

Another recruiter asked if she could help develop my website and invited me to speak at her company. A third said, "I have enjoyed speaking with you and learning about your skills and work history over the past couple of weeks while I've helped you search for a job. You are highly qualified for a senior-level executive position. ***However, when you told me your story it was just what I needed to hear. It has encouraged and motivated me.***"

Just when I thought she was going to send me on an interview, she dropped a bomb on me: "***It would be very selfish of you not to tell the world your story***. My recommendation is for you to do that as soon as possible."

I was so quiet she asked if I was still on the phone. I was, and after we wrapped up the conversation, she wished me well. ***Every door was shut except for the door God promised to open for me.*** The Lord was speaking to me clearly in undeniable ways. When would I be ready to obey Him?

It had been two years since I left my job.. I called Asa, who is a loving and patient man. When I talked to him about my hesitations, though, he was blunt. "Trust God, Joseph." Asa only calls me Joseph when he is unhappy with me!

"God has a plan for you," Asa said. "We can all see it, but *you* need to see it. How many times do we need to have this conversation?"

After that, I called my mentor. He reminded me of General George Washington's commitment to cross the Delaware River on Christmas Day in 1776. His decision foreshadowed the many hardships faced and the eventual victory of the Continental Army during the American Revolution. At first glance, the decision to transport 2,400 soldiers across an icy river on a dark, frigid night directly into a severe winter snowstorm seems irrational.

Washington's plan, however, relied on strategic motivation. He understood that the Continental Army desperately needed a victory after months of intense fighting with several significant defeats. He also understood that the element of surprise was the only way he and his army stood a chance of defeating the highly trained Hessian mercenaries.

On the morning of December 25, 1776, Continental soldiers woke up in their camps along the Delaware River to frozen, snow-covered ground. The weather worsened and the temperature continued to drop throughout the day. Late in the afternoon, the Continentals left their tents and began forming along the river in anticipation of the night's events. Washington kept almost all details of the crossing a secret; none of the soldiers knew anything about their upcoming mission.

Moving the troops on Christmas Day allowed his army to strike the Hessians at Trenton the next morning. The turning point came when Washington made a crucial decision to destroy his ships. It sent a powerful message to his men: *there is no turning back*. The general took an emphatic step of faith and was rewarded with a key victory for his army.

My mentor said, "If you are going to move forward and do what pleases God, you need to destroy your ship of safety."

My choice became so clear: continue clinging to the trust I had in my **experience** or take hold of God's promise to use the **gifts** He had given me.

I decided I was all in with God's plan.

As soon as I hung up the phone, I asked God to forgive me for not obeying Him and for not trusting His will for my life. I told the Lord that I chose to fully trust Him to accomplish His will for my life. Since that moment, there has been no turning back for me!

Trust in the Lord with all your heart and lean not on your own under-
standing; in all your ways acknowledge Him, and He will make your paths
straight. (Proverbs 3:5–6)

Looking back, I have no regrets. I know I am where God wants me to be. In God's presence I receive healing for my soul, strength, hope, joy, and protection. Best of all, I have peace and my fellowship with God is so sweet. This is what it means to be free in Christ Jesus!

A LEADER'S GREATEST NEED

I have talked with many CEOs, CFOs, senior executives, and pastors over the years. When they open up, most tell me how isolated they are. They describe feeling like empty people who have found a way to numb themselves just to get through the day. Buying new cars or bigger houses and making plenty of money will never fill this void. Abiding peace is what we all need.

We treat the role of a leader like that of a superhero. We expect our superheroes to come to the rescue day after day and year after year. Some leaders spend so much time rescuing people they have no time left to recharge. And their need to be rescued feels like failure to them.

This "leader as superhero" concept is problematic. When we elevate leaders and expect too much from them, we tend to forget that they have the same needs as everyone else. To keep up with a heavy load of demands, many of them are running on empty. Too often, leaders don't have the right people around them to keep their tanks full. Many people drain their tanks instead.

A lot of leaders don't have a safe place to share their struggles. Unfortunately, it's much easier to find a dangerous place with the wrong people and unhealthy habits. Without a safe place, it's hard for leaders to see how much help they desperately need.

What is a safe place? People we can *trust* and who don't think less of us when we open up and reveal our weaknesses or challenges. I use the word *weaknesses* intentionally, because most leaders have been taught not to use that word when talking about themselves. I just broke that rule! Often, breaking an irrational rule is what enables help and support. The *right* people in your safe place will tell you the hard and ugly truth when everyone else tells you how great you are.

Trustworthy people hold sensitive information in the highest confidence. They give wise counsel about taking care of yourself *first*. If you fail to take care of yourself, you will be a liability to the people you love most.

Think about a flight attendant's job. They tell passengers what to do in an emergency, and one of the first things they say is to place the oxygen mask over your face *before* trying to help anyone else. You can't help anyone unless you are safe and healthy. If you are distressed or in danger, you are a liability to everyone who depends upon you.

If you are an executive or a pastor, I pray that you will open your eyes and trust the people God has placed in your safe place to do life with you. They may not be the other leaders in your company or church, but I have learned from experience that God will never call you to be a leader without providing the right people in your safe place who will surround you with the support you need.

REFLECTION

Have you resisted, ignored, or delayed obeying God? I hope my story motivates you to seek His forgiveness and decide to do what He asks of you. What is holding you back?

_____

_____

_____

_____

_____

_____

_____

_____

_____

_____

_____

_____

_____

_____

_____

_____

_____

_____

_____

_____

_____

CHAPTER # 9
ACCEPTING YOUR ASSIGNMENT

The [reverent] fear of the Lord [that is, worshiping Him and regarding Him as truly awesome] is the beginning and the preeminent part of wisdom [its starting point and its essence], And the knowledge of the Holy One is understanding and spiritual insight. (Proverbs 9:10, Amplified Bible)

When my daughter was growing up, I had to teach her to look both ways before she crossed a parking lot or a street. Danielle wasn't born knowing cars can seriously injure her if she doesn't watch where she is walking. But after I instructed her to be careful and to hold my hand when she needed help navigating a busy place, I expected her to obey me so she would be safe. Since Danielle knew I loved her, she wanted to please me by taking my hand.

Trusting, obeying, and wanting to please God are the keys to unlocking what it means to have a "reverent fear" of the Lord. We become wise when we recognize that God always has our best interest in mind and expects us to listen to Him. Just as I want my daughter to be safe, God wants us to be safe. Even more than that, He wants us to cooperate with Him.

Just as I had to teach Danielle to obey me, God teaches His children to obey Him. Our human nature wants to go its own way, but a healthy fear of the consequences for disobeying motivates us to make the right choice. As we grow, we begin to recognize the wisdom and the love behind what God requires of us. Eventually, we find comfort in His sovereignty over all things, including His children.

To accept my assignment from the Lord, I had to get at a place of total submission. I had to trust God to do what He said He would do. As you have followed my journey, you've seen how often the people around me saw clearly what God was doing and believed His promises to me, even when I struggled to see and believe.

I had to come to complete obedience before I felt free and at peace about accepting my assignment from God. As I spend quality time with God, cooperating with Him is less about fearing the consequence of not obeying and more about looking forward to the blessings of living in the center of His will. Only good can come from doing what God asks of me, not just for myself but for others too.

We suffer when we don't listen to God. We see this in the Bible stories about Jacob, King David, and Jonah. But like the great men and women of God, we learn through experience that the Lord's will is the best path to walk.

No doubt, if I had obeyed God sooner than I did, the road would have been easier for my family and me. But I realize that the Lord was preparing me to carry out my assignment even when I was dragging my feet. Nothing compares to the peace I now have knowing that I am faithfully doing what He asks of me and honoring what He has entrusted to me.

WORKING ON MY ASSIGNMENT

After I humbled myself and totally submitted to God, the doors with the *right* opportunities started opening. I currently have a robust consulting relationship with a Fortune 500 company in which I lead an initiative to mentor and develop leadership programs that help youth living in poverty in some of the neediest areas of our nation's cities. Getting involved with communities and neighborhoods like the one I grew up in is a dream come true. I get to build programs that offer hope, encouragement, and important life skills to young people. Lives and families are being uplifted, and the positive changes will bless generations to come. Best of all, I get to share Christ wherever I go. This includes the other speaking engagements I do throughout the US. Running corporations was never this rewarding!

GOD HAS AN ASSIGNMENT FOR YOU

Each of us has an appointment with God that we cannot cancel or reschedule; on that day, we must give account to Him. It will be our final exam. Since He loves us as a good Father, He's already given us the answers we need to pass the exam. Will you go to Him for the answers ***before*** you need them?

Jesus left us with these explicit instructions in the Great Commission:

> *Then the eleven disciples went to Galilee, to the mountain where Jesus had told them to go. When they saw him, they worshiped Him; but some doubted. Then Jesus came to them and said, "All authority in heaven and on earth has been given to me. Therefore go and make disciples of all nations, baptizing them in the name of the Father and of the Son and of the Holy Spirit, And teaching them to obey everything I have commanded you. And surely I am with you always, to the very end of the age." (Matthew 28:16–20)*

To please God, you must accept your assignment *and* complete it. Each of us has unique talents and gifts that enable us to undertake our assignments, and we have different approaches to getting things done. But every assignment from God has three basic components we must act upon: 1) accept the mandate to go; 2) count the cost; and 3) introduce people to Christ.

1. Accept the Mandate to Go

As born-again believers, we are the body of Christ, and Jesus is the Head of this body (Colossians 1:18). As His body, the assignment Jesus had during His ministry on Earth is now our assignment. The apostle Paul described born-again believers as ambassadors of Christ (2 Corinthians 5:20). We go forth in His name and carry His message to the world in order to continue what He started.

This is how Jesus described His assignment:

The Spirit of the Lord is on me, because He has anointed me to proclaim good news to the poor. He has sent me to proclaim freedom for the prisoners and recovery of sight for the blind, to set the oppressed free, to proclaim the year of the Lord's favor. (Luke 4:18)

Jesus calls us not only to come to Him but also to go for Him. He was clear when He said, "As the Father has sent Me, I am sending you."

The Great Commission is a responsibility of every follower of Jesus, not just pastors and missionaries. It is not the Great Suggestion. ***This commission is not optional for any Christian.*** Ignoring or sidestepping the Great Commission is disobeying the Lord.

The Bible says, "You must warn them so they may live" (Ezekiel 3:18). If you don't warn the wicked to stop their evil ways, they will die in their sins. Christians have a responsibility to tell people the truth. You might be the only Christian some people will ever know, and your assignment is to share the good news of Jesus with them. Telling others how they can have eternal life is the greatest gift you can ever give them.

The consequences of ***not*** carrying out our assignments will last forever. Nothing else we do matters as much as leading people to an eternal relationship with God. If you discovered the cure for cancer, would you keep it to yourself? Of course not! You would tell everyone within reach about this good news. How much more valuable to this world is the good news of eternal life in Christ Jesus?

The fruit of the righteous is a tree of life, and he who wins souls is wise. (Proverbs 11:30)

Jesus said, "The Good News about God's kingdom will be preached in the entire world, to every nation, then the end will come" (Matthew 24:14). It is easy to get distracted and lose focus on what really matters. Satan knows this and wants to see us busy doing anything other than sharing our faith.

*Do not store up for yourselves treasures on earth, where moths and vermin destroy, and where thieves break in and steal. But store up for yourselves treasures in heaven, where moths and vermin do not destroy, and where thieves do not break in and steal. **For where your treasure is, there your heart will be also.** (Matthew 6:19–21)*

Obeying God's command requires that you trade your agenda for God's agenda. All of us must come clean with God and accept His will for our lives while surrendering our will to Him. Looking at this from the flip side, embracing God's will for your life means embracing His best intentions for you. God wants all His children to live and move within the center of His will for each of us. In that place we are safe, our needs are taken care of, and we enjoy God's peace.

In Your presence is fullness of joy. (Psalm 16:11)

2. Count the Cost

Once we accept our assignment to carry out the Great Commission, we need to understand that there is a cost to carrying it out. When Jesus asked the disciples to follow Him, they left behind all they had. Even Judas, the betrayer, left everything to follow Christ. *His failure was refusing to give Jesus his heart.* Judas had an outward devotion to Jesus, but the Lord wanted inward conversion. If love is not our motivation for serving Christ, we won't please Him.

Luke gave us a clear picture of how costly it could be to withhold ourselves from Christ:

> *As they were walking along the road, a man said to Him, I will follow you wherever you go. Jesus replied, "Foxes have holes and birds of the air have nests, but the Son of Man has no place to lay his head." He said to another man, "Follow me." But the man replied, "Lord, first let me go bury my father." Jesus said to him, "Let the dead bury their own dead, but go and proclaim the kingdom of God." Still another said, "I will follow you, Lord; but first let me go back and say goodbye to my family." Jesus replied, "No one who puts his hands to the plow and looks back is fit for service in the kingdom of God." (Luke 9:57–62)*

Jesus will never ask you to forsake your responsibilities to your family, but you must be ready to serve Him even if it requires sacrifice on your part.

3. **Introduce People to Christ**

When someone begins a relationship with Jesus, they go from being an enemy of God to His friend (Romans 5:10). Even better than friendship, God promises to adopt those who obey Him as His sons (Romans 8:14–17). The Lord wants to add children to His kingdom, and we get to help Him do this. God wants us to join in with His plan to redeem humanity from sin and death by uniting them to Christ.

By accepting Christ as Savior, we join God's family. We should love Him, serve Him, and tell others about Him. Once we receive salvation, God uses us to reach others. *He saves us and then sends us out.*

There are many ways we can introduce people to Christ. If we lead by example through a Christ-like life, we will find many opportunities to introduce Jesus to the people within our sphere of influence. Whether it's at work or serving our communities or even at home, expressing God's love with our words and actions is a powerful way to draw people to the Lord. Conversations are important. People often have many questions about Jesus. We can invite people to coffee or lunch to have one-to-one chats. We can also invite them to church or to a Bible study group. Christian mission trips allow us to share our faith throughout the world.

The apostle Paul gives us a wonderful example of someone who took his assignment seriously. After he met Jesus, he spent the rest of his life carrying the gospel to anyone who would listen. Many times they rejected him. But that did not stop him. Despite the costs and the trials, Paul served the Lord with gladness and gratitude. He never forgot that he was a sinner saved by Jesus. He owed his life to God. Paul wrote many of the New Testament letters, where he encouraged the body of Christ to obey God and spread the good news of the gospel. The book of Acts tells the story of Paul's life as a sinner who persecuted Christians, repented and was saved, and faithfully completed his assignments for the Lord.

I have fought a good fight, I have finished my course, I have kept the faith: Henceforth there is laid up for me a crown of righteousness, which the Lord, the righteous Judge, shall give me at that day: and not to me only, but unto all them also that love His appearing. (2 Timothy 4:7–8)

REFLECTION

What are some practical ways you can act on the assignments God has given you? Write them below and pray through them.

_____

_____

_____

_____

_____

_____

_____

_____

_____

_____

_____

_____

_____

_____

_____

_____

_____

_____

_____

_____

_____

_____

CHAPTER # 10
CLOSING WORDS

If I could go back in time, I would put my arms around that little boy sitting on the steps of 3C Lee Walker Heights dreaming. I would tell him not to worry and let him know everything is going be alright because God has a plan for his life. If I could, I would encourage him to stay the course regardless of his circumstances because God loves and cares for him.

Since it is impossible for me to go back in time and comfort little Joe, I want to spend the rest of my life telling little boys and girls, men and women that God has a plan for their lives and loves them more than they can comprehend!

Remember, Jesus is the Author and Finisher of our story. We must be good stewards over the story He entrusts to us.

Thank you for taking the time to read about my journey from the projects to the boardroom. I pray that God uses my story to encourage, inspire, bring hope, and help people dealing with unforgiveness begin the process of forgiving others.

Most important, my prayer is that this story will lead people to accept Christ as their Savior and obey Him as the King of kings.

I would not trade my assignment for anything the world has to offer!

A line from Josh Baldwin's "Evidence," one of my favorite songs, sums it up perfectly for me: **"I see the evidence of Your goodness all over my life."**

If you would like to learn more about my story, go to www.3CLead.com.

Please contact me at joe@3clead.com if you want to invite me to speak at your company, event, or church.

ABOUT THE AUTHOR

Joseph Humphries is a senior-level executive specializing in crisis management and turnarounds of distressed companies. Being an engaged, effective leader has allowed him to galvanize organizations around a common purpose while driving profitable business growth and sustainable change.

Joe has successfully led businesses through seasons of significant disruption, conflict, and cultural transformation. By assembling and coaching the right stakeholders, his teams surpass their business objectives. The results have been measured in hundreds of millions of dollars saved through improved operations.

After thirty-two years Joe left corporate America in a step of faith to answer God's call to share his story of hope, healing, and encouragement with a wider audience. His passion to coach, train leaders, and inspire people comes from a life spent overcoming challenges. As a boy growing up in public housing in Asheville, NC, Joe clearly remembers the many times he sat on the front steps of apartment 3C dreaming of a better future for himself and his family.

Joe's story is about working hard, staying the course, and trusting God's favor—the same things that took him from the projects to the boardroom, leading companies all over the world and turning them into profitable corporations. Joe has spoken at governors' events, CEO luncheons, national annual sales meetings, corporate team-building retreats, fundraising events, youth and athletic events, prisons, and churches.

Joe completed executive education programs at Massachusetts Institute of Technology (MIT) Sloan School of Management and the University of Wisconsin-Madison School of Business. He also undertook Executive Leadership Training at the Center for Creative Leadership in Greensboro, NC.

For Joe, dedication to business success is equal to his commitment to community service. Believing in the importance of volunteerism drives him to lead by example. Joe served his church as a deacon and outreach leader for many years. He also served for a six-year term as a sitting elder at Crossroads Fellowship Church in Raleigh, NC. For five years Joe was a colonel in the "We Build People Program" at his local YMCA. He has served as an advisory board member for the North Carolina State Employees Credit Union (SECU) and for Lighthouse Ministry, a Christian counseling service; he has also served on several corporate boards. Joe is currently on the board of directors for Church Initiative, a Christian publishing company, and is an advisory board member for TradeUP Career. He often gives back to the community by mentoring, coaching, and teaching life skills. Joe received an award from the state of North Carolina, presented by the governor, for his dedication and devotion to volunteer service.

Joe lives in North Carolina with his wife of thirty-four years, Janet. They are the proud parents of Danielle, who graduated from Liberty University.